QUICK and EASY Devotions for Youth Groups

Volume I

compiled and edited by

MICHAEL WARDEN

Group

Loveland, Colorado

QUICK AND EASY DEVOTIONS FOR YOUTH GROUPS, VOLUME I

Copyright © 1995 Group Publishing, Inc.

CREDITS

Contributing Authors: Chip Borgstadt, Jim Feldbush, Pam Montgomery, Stephen Parolini, James Selman, Jane Vogel, Gary Wilde, Beth Wolf, and Christine Yount
Book Acquisitions Editor: Mike Nappa
Editors: Michael Warden and Jan Kershner
Senior Editor: Dan Benson
Creative Products Director: Joani Schultz
Copy Editor: Sandra Collier
Art Director: Lisa Chandler
Cover Art Director: Liz Howe
Designer: Bill Fisher
Computer Graphic Artist: Bill Fisher
Cover Illustrator: DeWain Stoll
Illustrators: Abe Gurvin and Layne Petersen
Production Manager: Gingar Kunkel

Unless otherwise noted, Scriptures quoted from The Youth Bible, New Century Version, copyright © 1991 by Word Publishing, Dallas, Texas 75039. Used by permission.

Library of Congress Cataloging-in-Publication Data
Quick and easy devotions for youth groups / compiled and edited by Michael Warden.
           p.   cm.
    Includes indexes.
    ISBN 1-55945-701-5 (v. 1)
    1. Youth—Prayer-books and devotions—English. 2. Church group work with youth. I. Warden, Michael D.
BV4850.Q53 1995
242'.63—dc20
                                    95-626
                                       CIP

Printed in the United States of America.
10 9 8 7 6 5 4 3 2 1   04 03 02 01 00 99 98 97 96 95

CONTENTS

SCENE 2: *Looking at Our World*

Contents

SCENE 3: *Looking at Our Special Days*

Contents

Introduction

There's a reason you're reading this introduction.

If you're like thousands of youth leaders across the nation, it's because you're looking for new, exciting ways to help the teenagers in your youth group grow closer to God.

And you want to know that those ways *work*. No pie-in-the-sky activities that sound great on paper and flop royally in real life.

And you want those ideas to be quick and easy to use—each one taking about 10 to 15 minutes in your youth meeting. (After all, when was the last time you bought a book titled, *Really Long and Complicated Ideas for Youth Ministry That Take Forever to Understand and Even Longer to Actually Do?*)

Well, you've come to the right place. Because there's a reason we wrote this introduction (and this book)!

Quick and Easy Devotions for Youth Groups, Volume I will provide you with new, exciting ways to help the teenagers in your youth group grow closer to God. And we've made sure each devotion in this book was written by an experienced youth worker like you.

And we've made sure that each devotion is quick—designed to make a major impact in a short amount of time. Since each devotion lasts about 15 minutes, you can use them to enliven a lesson, spice up a youth talk, wrap up a meeting, add depth to a retreat, spark discussion in a small-group Bible study, or bring new meaning to any activity with teenagers.

And we've made sure that each devotion can be ready in minutes—no confusing directions or complicated preparation involved. (Hey, we didn't call this book *Quick and Easy Devotions for Youth*

Groups for nothing.)

The devotions in this book touch on real-life issues that are important to the teenagers in your group. You'll find timely topics such as self-identity, relationships, stress, and fear, all covered from a biblical perspective, all firmly rooted in Scripture.

Imagine your youth ministry is the set of a blockbuster movie, then use this book to "direct" your kids in a meaningful learning experience. Whether you're a seasoned producer or a newcomer to the cast, you'll find this book a valuable tool for leading kids into a deeper relationship with God.

LIGHTS... CAMERA... ACTION!

Don't take the stage without a script! Take a minute to read through the following highlights. Each devotion in *Quick and Easy Devotions for Youth Groups* consists of the following elements:

TOPIC—*This is the main theme of the devotion. Each theme was chosen to address a topic of particular interest or concern to today's teenagers.*

SCRIPTURE—*You'll find the main Scripture reference for each devotion listed in this section. Every devotion in this book helps teenagers focus on at least one passage of Scripture. Learning that the Bible addresses every area of their lives will help kids turn to God on a daily basis.*

SYNOPSIS—*Here's a quick, concise description of what you can expect to happen during the devotion.*

BEHIND THE SCENES—*This brief section tells you exactly how to prepare for the devotion. It explains any supplies or preparation that may be involved.*

While each devotion is designed to be ready in minutes with a minimum of effort, you may want to check out this section before your meeting. Involving kids in the preparation can make the devotion more meaningful and is an especially good way to involve shy or distant kids in the fun.

ACTION! Just as a good movie involves its audience, each devotion actively involves your teenagers. Kids will experience the theme by using their senses of sight, touch, smell, and taste. As a result, the theme will be imprinted on their hearts, much like images on film.

Feel free to adapt any of these quick devotions to fit your group's size and personality. If your group is particularly large, have kids break into small groups for discussion. If you have shy kids or frequent newcomers, use the quick devotion on friendship as an icebreaker each time you meet. If your group is studying a special subject, begin and end your time together with devotions relating to that topic.

CLOSE UP! Zoom in on the devotion's message and bring it into clear focus for your kids with this section of deeper development. Help kids analyze the action, discuss their reactions, and share insights. You'll be surprised at the growth your group will make.

It's a Wrap! Every devotion concludes with a powerful activity to help kids apply what they've discovered. This important segment makes sure kids don't leave what they've learned at the church door!

AND THE WINNER IS...

You...and your teenagers...and the kids they come in contact with. We've made sure that the devotions in this book will touch, teach, and test the teenagers in your care.

We're confident this star-studded collection of quick and easy devotions will become a trusted friend to you in the days to come. Now, why don't you take a few moments to get better acquainted?

Scene 1:
Looking at Our Faith

LISTEN UP!

- **TOPIC:** *Beginning a relationship with God*
- **SCRIPTURE:** *Psalm 46:10*
- **SYNOPSIS:** *Group members will learn that building a relationship with God involves learning to listen.*
- **BEHIND THE SCENES:** *You'll need Bibles.*

 **ACTION!**

Say: **Today we're going to learn each other's life histories.**

Form trios and have each group sit in a circle. On "go," have kids simultaneously begin telling each other about their lives. Encourage kids to talk louder than their trio members so they alone can be heard.

After a minute gather all the kids together. Ask: **What did you learn about the others in your group? How did you feel trying to make everyone else hear your story? Did you try to listen to their stories while you talked? Why or why not? How do you think God feels if we "shout" requests at him and never take time to listen to him by meditating on his Word? Why might it be important to just sit quietly at times and listen for God to speak to us?**

Looking at Our Faith

 **CLOSE UP!** Have kids return to their trios and read Psalm 46:10. After they've read the verse, have them discuss these questions in their groups: **What are some ways we can be still and listen for God's voice? How can we recognize God's voice speaking to us personally through the Bible? Why do we often have such a hard time just being still and listening for God's voice?**

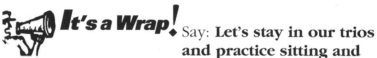 **It's a Wrap!** Say: **Let's stay in our trios and practice sitting and listening quietly right now.**

Have each trio member tell of one exciting incident in his or her life. Instruct the other two trio members to say nothing but just listen carefully to the story being told.

To close, have each kid repeat one of the stories he or she heard in the group.

IT'S ALL GREEK TO ME

- **TOPIC:** *Bible study*
- **SCRIPTURE:** *1 Corinthians 2:12-14*
- **SYNOPSIS:** *Group members will learn that*

without the Holy Spirit's help they can't understand the real message of the Bible.

● **BEHIND THE SCENES:** *You'll need a sheet of paper for each person with the following code written on it: bjdt;st3kd5 d83md8fjw5 93jgkd54ikt0 (or any other random group of letters and numbers). You'll also need pencils and Bibles for everyone.*

 **ACTION!**

Say: **Today we're going to work on a very unusual puzzle.**

Form pairs. Hand each pair a pencil and a copy of the coded message. Then say: **I'll give you five minutes to see if you can "crack the code."**

After five minutes, assemble the group again and ask for any guesses. After everyone has had a chance to guess, say: **As far as I know, there isn't an answer to this code. The combination of letters and numbers is totally random. But we don't have to leave it to chance when it comes to the Holy Spirit.**

Ask: **What was frustrating about trying to figure out the code? How was that like trying to figure out the Bible sometimes? What would have helped you crack the code? Why do we need help to understand Scriptures?**

CLOSE UP! Have the pairs form groups of four. Ask groups to read 1 Corinthians 2:12-14. Then have kids discuss the following questions in their groups: **Why do people sometimes find the Bible boring? Why do people sometimes have a hard time sticking with Bible study? According to this passage, what's required for us to understand the Bible. How does the Holy Spirit help us understand God's Word? What are some things you can do to improve your ability to hear God speak through his Word?**

After each question and discussion, have the small groups report their answers to the whole group.

It's a Wrap! Have everyone find a partner, then say: **Tell your partner what you'll do this week to get to know God better through the study of his Word. For example, you could meditate on one psalm all week or read about all the times Christ used the word "forgive."**

After partners have shared their ideas, say: **Now pray together and ask God to open your eyes to the wonders of his Word.**

NOT THIS AGAIN!

- **TOPIC:** *Boredom*
- **SCRIPTURE:** *Colossians 3:23*
- **SYNOPSIS:** *Group members will explore boredom and learn the value of doing their best at whatever they do.*
- **BEHIND THE SCENES:** *You'll need paper and Bibles.*

 **ACTION!** Give each kid five sheets of paper. Then say: **For the next five minutes, you'll each have a very special assignment—to stack your papers, then spread them out on the floor, then restack them** (as many times as you want)**.**

Tell the kids to be silent during this activity and to follow the instructions as best they can. Tell kids to begin and watch to make sure each person is complying with the instructions.

After five minutes (it'll seem like five hours), call time. Form trios and have kids discuss the following questions in their groups: **What feelings did you experience during this activity? What made this activity boring? What things in life bore you most? How do you usually react when you're bored?**

CLOSE UP! Have a volunteer from each trio share insights from his or her group's discussion. Then read aloud Colossians 3:23. Ask: **How does this verse apply to boredom? Is it possible to "give your all" to God when you're bored? How does living for God change the way you feel about boring times? What are ways to make boring times more exciting?**

Have trio members stack their papers together one at a time. As each sheet of paper is placed, have that trio member suggest a good way to make boring activities more exciting, such as dancing while vacuuming the floors or making bubbles while doing the dishes. After trios have stacked all their papers, have a volunteer from each group share their best ideas.

It's a Wrap! Say: **Boredom is a part of every person's life. But we can overcome boredom by doing our best for God in everything we do.**

Have each kid take a sheet of paper. Tell kids to write their names on them along with a list of two or three fun, productive things to do the next time they're bored. When the lists have been completed, have volunteers close with a prayer asking God to help the group members come up with creative solutions to boredom.

Looking at Our Faith

FROM THE INSIDE OUT!

- **TOPIC:** *Discovering God's will*
- **SCRIPTURE:** *Romans 12:2*
- **SYNOPSIS:** *Group members will make cookies and explore the difference between being like the world on the outside and being changed to be like God from the inside.*
- **BEHIND THE SCENES:** *You'll need Bibles, prepared cookie dough, baking supplies, cookie cutters (preferably people shapes), baking sheets, and a place to bake the cookies.*

 **ACTION!** Set out the cookie dough, baking supplies, cookie cutters, and baking sheets, then ask kids to work together to make the cookies.

While the cookies are baking, have kids each describe what their "dream cookie" would be like. Encourage them to include details of size, shape, and flavor. Then ask: **What makes thinking about your own personal dream cookie fun? How is your dream cookie unique? What makes you unique as a person? How is making cookies with a cookie cutter like peer pressure? What's your reaction when you see everyone wearing new designer tennis shoes? sporting a new hairstyle? wearing new clothes? Even though we all want to be unique, why is "fitting in" important to us?**

CLOSE UP! Have kids sit in a circle, then have a volunteer read Romans 12:2 aloud. Ask: **The word "transform" means to change from one thing to another; how are we "transformed" as Christians? How can being transformed make us different from people who give in to peer pressure? How does being transformed by God help us discover his will for our lives? When has God shown his will for your life by transforming your attitude or personality?**

It's a Wrap! When the cookies have cooled, let the kids begin to snack. Say: **If all we ate were cookies, pretty soon we'd all be changed "from the inside out" to reflect what we eat. Our Christian walk is like that, too (only not as fattening). As we learn more about God through his Word, he changes us from the inside out and shows us his will for our lives.**

Close by having kids share with partners one way they see God's will being worked out in their lives.

THE BIG FREEZE

- **TOPIC:** *Faithfulness*
- **SCRIPTURE:** *Proverbs 25:13; 1 Corinthians 15:58, 16:13; Hebrews 10:23-25; and 1 Peter 5:8-11*

- **SYNOPSIS:** *Group members will hold ice cubes until they melt and discover why being faithful to God requires endurance.*
- **BEHIND THE SCENES:** *You'll need ice, a towel, soft drinks, paper cups, paper, pencils, and Bibles.*

ACTION! Hand each kid an ice cube. Have kids hold their ice cubes in the palm of one of their hands until it melts. Tell students not to pass the ice back and forth between their hands.

While the ice is melting, say: **Now let's worship God.**

Sing quiet, meditative songs such as "Sing Hallelujah to the Lord," "Alleluia," and "God Is So Good" until everyone's ice cube has melted.

Pass around the towel and have everyone dry their hands.

Ask: **How did your hand feel during this activity? What did you think about while we were singing? Did you consider giving up? Why or why not? What convinced you to stick with it? How was the discomfort you felt during this activity like striving to be faithful to God at all times?**

CLOSE UP! Form three groups. Have one group look up 1 Corinthians 15:58 and 16:13 and discuss: **What are the rewards of faithfulness? What happens**

when Christians aren't faithful?

Have the second group look up 1 Peter 5:8-11 and discuss: **What aid can Christians expect to help them remain faithful?**

Have the third group look up Hebrews 10:23-25 and discuss: **What specific things can we do to help each other remain faithful?**

After discussions, give each group a moment to share its discoveries with the rest of the class.

 **It's a Wrap!** Fill paper cups with ice and soft drinks. Give each person a cup. Read Proverbs 25:13 from the New American Standard Version. Say: **As you drink, think of one way that you can be faithful to God this week. Imagine how God will feel refreshed by your faithfulness.**

After you've enjoyed the cool drinks, have volunteers share how they'll be faithful in the coming week.

SCARED OF SOAKING?

- ● **TOPIC:** *Fears*
- ● **SCRIPTURE:** *Matthew 14:22-33*
- ● **SYNOPSIS:** *Group members will explore the relationship between fear and the ability to trust.*
- ● **BEHIND THE SCENES:** *Prepare one small*

water balloon for each person. You'll also need a needle, paper strips, markers or crayons, pieces of string, and a Bible.

 **ACTION!** Have everyone sit in a circle and place a water balloon in each person's lap. Ask: **How many of you believe you won't get wet today? How many of you are afraid you might get wet?** Ask for a show of hands, then produce a needle and show it to everyone.

Say: **Whether your fears about getting soaked are justified all depends on trust: How much are you willing to trust your friends?**

Hand the needle to a person in the circle and tell the group members that they must pass the needle slowly around the circle. The only movement they can make is to take the needle in one hand and pass it to their neighbor. The catch: To make the transfer, they must lay the needle on top of their neighbor's balloon!

 **CLOSE UP!** When the needle has completed the circle (whether or not anyone has gotten wet), gather the group and have a volunteer read aloud Matthew 14:22-33.

Ask: **How did you feel having to trust someone with a needle near your balloon? How does dealing with our fears help us to trust others? trust God? When has some form of trust helped you to overcome a fear? What happened?**

Say: **Peter started out full of confidence, but before too long, he became afraid of getting wet! Our fears can do that to us—make us lose our confidence. Most likely, a big part of Peter's fear was his uncertainty about whether Jesus was trustworthy. Would Jesus let him down?**

It's a Wrap! Say: **Let's symbolically smash a few of our fears right now—as a reminder to trust Jesus to help us overcome fear in the future.**

Distribute strips of paper, string, and markers, and invite everyone to draw a symbol on the paper representing the greatest fear in their lives right now. When everyone has tied a "fear-symbol" to a balloon, go outside and, in one grand, splashy finale, throw the balloons high into the air.

GOD'S POWERFUL GRIP

- **TOPIC:** *God's love*
- **SCRIPTURE:** *Romans 8:35-39*
- **SYNOPSIS:** *Group members will explore the differences between the bond of human relationships and God's love.*
- **BEHIND THE SCENES:** *You'll need a Chinese finger-handcuff from a toy shop (as shown on the following page) and a Bible.*

ACTION!

Form two groups. Ask both groups to stand and form circles. Have group members put their right hands into the center of the circle and hold the right hands of the people across from them. Then say: **We are now "tight" with each other. We have two "human webs" of closeness and love.**

Have kids use their free hands to lock arms with kids in the other group. Tell kids their task is to hold their own group together while trying to pull the other group out of their "web." After a few minutes, stop the activity and congratulate the winning group.

CLOSE UP!

Ask: **What was it like for you to be so physically close to others? What was your reaction to being pulled away from your group? to pulling others away from their group? How is this experience similar to what happens to love and friendship in real life? How does it make you feel knowing that a lot of your relationships today probably won't last?**

Read Romans 8:35-39 aloud. Say: **Human fellowship can be very close and rewarding. But we can be separated and pulled apart for all kinds of reasons (by death, for instance). Yet God's love never, ever "loses its grip" on us.**

Ask: **Do you have trouble believing God's love will never fail you? Why or why not? How can we overcome our tendency to believe God's love for us is like human love? How would your life be different if you never doubted God's love for you?**

It's a Wrap!

Take out the Chinese handcuff and put it on your finger. Say: **Theoretically, it's impossible for me to be separated from anyone who puts their finger in the other end of this handcuff.**

Invite a volunteer to insert a finger in the other end of the handcuff. Then both of you pull. Say: **This is just like God's love for us. Even when we pull away—because of our ignorance or sin—God's love tightens on us, and no power can separate us. Let's spend a moment praying for someone we know who needs that kind of love: a friend, relative, an enemy—or even ourselves.**

After kids have prayed silently, close by reading Romans 8:35-39 again.

BRUISED SOULS

- **TOPIC:** *Healing life's hurts*
- **SCRIPTURE:** *2 Corinthians 1:3-7*
- **SYNOPSIS:** *Group members will discover how God's compassion flows from those who've been comforted by him.*
- **BEHIND THE SCENES:** *You'll need a blue and a black marker for every two people. You'll also need a Bible.*

 **ACTION!** Ask kids to find partners and hand each pair a blue and a black marker. Say: **Turn your back to your partner and draw a "hurt" on yourself—a black-and-blue wound or bruise. Make sure the wound is in a place where your partner can't see it.**

When both partners have made a black-and-blue hurt, say: **Now your task is to find out where your partner is hurting. You can only do this by holding your elbow near your partner and moving it as you receive feedback: "More hurtin'" or "Less hurtin'."**

Offer a prize for the first five people to locate their partners' hurts.

CLOSE UP! Ask: **What was it like for you to try to find your partner's hurt? How is this experience like trying to find out where someone is hurting inside? What's the hardest thing about finding out where a friend is hurting? In your opinion, what's the best way to help heal a wounded person?**

Ask someone to read 2 Corinthians 1:3-7 aloud, then repeat verses 3-5. Say: **When we hurt, our healing can come from God's comfort. But God's comfort often flows through other people who've overcome wounds just like ours.**

Have kids turn to a partner and ask:

● When have you found this to be true in your life?

● How have you helped someone else with a hurt you've experienced yourself?

● Why do you think God set up life that way—so that our "pain" ends up being someone else's "gain"?

It's a Wrap! Have partners tell each other about a real hurt in their lives, then pray together for God to send loving people to help heal their hurts.

HOLY! HOLY! HOLY!

- **TOPIC:** *Holiness*
- **SCRIPTURE:** *Isaiah 6:1-7*
- **SYNOPSIS:** *Group members will see "invisible" writing "revealed" as it's placed near a light and learn about God's holiness.*
- **BEHIND THE SCENES:** *Write the word "holy" on one sheet of white paper using lemon juice. You'll also need a hot light source, a Bible, and two sheets of blank white paper for each kid.*

 **ACTION!**

Give each kid a sheet of blank paper then ask: **What do you think happens when we draw near to God?**

Say: **Do to your paper something that represents what you think happens when we try to draw near to God.** Give them an example, such as tearing the paper to show that we feel torn between God and what other people want us to do.

When kids have finished, have them explain to the group what they've made. Then hold up the paper you wrote on and the light source and say: **If this paper represents my life and this light source represents God, let's see if bringing them together will show us anything.**

Hold up the paper to the light source. The heat will activate the lemon juice and reveal the word "holy." After kids read the word, ask: **What do you think this means?**

CLOSE UP!

Read Isaiah 6:1-5 aloud. Ask: **What happened to Isaiah? What happened to the sheet of paper when it came near the light?**

Say: **The Bible says that God is light. He is holy. As we draw near to God, our unholiness is revealed and our sin is taken away.**

Read aloud Isaiah 6:6-7. Ask: **What does God do for us so we can be in his presence? Will we ever be as holy as God? Why or why not?**

It's a Wrap!

Give each kid a new sheet of paper. Say: **God is holy and perfect. If we compare ourselves to God, we'll never measure up. But God sent Jesus Christ to forgive our sins and to help us stand before God. As we close, shape this new sheet of paper into something that represents how you feel about what Jesus did on the cross.** (Give them an example, such as shaping the paper into a smile to show they're happy that Jesus loved them that much.)

When kids have finished, close with prayer.

FLOCK BUSTERS

- **TOPIC:** *Jesus the Good Shepherd*
- **SCRIPTURE:** *John 10:1-18*
- **SYNOPSIS:** *Group members will try to follow a particular sound among many then discuss what it means to listen to Jesus' voice.*
- **BEHIND THE SCENES:** *You'll need paper grocery sacks, Bibles, paper, and pencils. You'll also need three cotton balls for each person.*

 **ACTION!** Have kids put paper grocery sacks over their heads so that they can't see. Say: **I'm going to whisper to you the name of an animal. On "go," make the sound that animal makes. Move around the room and try to find the other people making the same animal sound.**

Assign animal names so that you have three of each kind of animal. Say "go," and let the "animals" find one another.

 **CLOSE UP!** Have kids take off the sacks and stay in their trios. Hand out Bibles, pencils, and paper. Have each trio appoint one person to read the Bible passage, one to record the trio's responses to the

questions, and one to report their answers.

Ask: **How did you feel when you were trying to find your animal group? Explain.**

Have the reader in each trio read John 10:1-18 aloud. Ask: **How are the sheep in this passage like you were during this activity? What are some of the benefits for sheep when they listen to their shepherd? What are some of the benefits for us when we listen to Jesus? What other voices try to distract us from hearing Jesus' voice? How can following Jesus the Good Shepherd help you this week? How might following Jesus the Good Shepherd challenge you this week?**

Say: **Sheep tend to stick together. Where one goes, they all go. That can be a good thing if they're going in the right direction but a bad thing if they're going into danger.**

Ask: **What are some ways we can "flock together" to encourage each other to go the right way?**

Have each reporter share his or her trio's responses.

It's a Wrap! Give each person three cotton balls. Say: **It's time to give the people in your trio some "warm fuzzies." Tell your partners one way you have seen each of them be a good influence, helping the "sheep" in the right direction, then give that person a cotton ball. When everyone in your trio has done that, put your third cotton ball in the center of your trio and say a one-sentence prayer thanking or praising Jesus for being our Good Shepherd.**

Looking at Our Faith

RULES AS TOOLS

- **TOPIC:** *Obedience*
- **SCRIPTURE:** *Romans 8:34-39 and Colossians 3:22-24*
- **SYNOPSIS:** *Group members will follow directions in a game and explore the attitude of obedience.*
- **BEHIND THE SCENES:** *You'll need Bibles.*

 **ACTION!** Say: **Let's play a game similar to Simon Says. The leader will give the class a series of directions to obey. Directions might include instructions such as "Hop on your right foot three times" or "Do 10 jumping jacks."** Choose one kid to lead the game. Tell the class they'll have to listen carefully to the leader's directions. If the leader begins a direction with his or her name, such as "Whitney says," the class should obey the directions. If the leader omits his or her name, the class shouldn't obey.

Anyone who obeys a direction not preceded by the leader's name is out of the game and must sit down until the game is finished. Play a few rounds of the game if time permits, choosing a new leader each time.

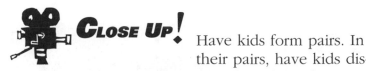

CLOSE UP! Have kids form pairs. In their pairs, have kids discuss the following questions then share their insights with the rest of the class.

Ask: **Why was it hard to follow the directions correctly each time? How was playing this game like following God's "directions"? What was it like to have to stop playing the game after you obeyed the wrong direction? How was being separated from the game like what happens when we don't obey God?**

Form trios. Have kids read Colossians 3:22-24 together then discuss the following questions in their groups: **How do you feel when someone tells you to do something you don't want to do? What makes taking directions from one person different from taking them from another? Why is it hard to take directions from your teachers? from your parents? from God? Why do you think God cares what we do?**

Have partners tell each other one step they will take toward becoming more obedient to God this week.

It's a Wrap! Have kids form a circle, then read Romans 8:34-39 aloud. Ask kids to take turns sharing one way God has shown his love to them this week.

After everyone has shared, say: **Our lives are always secure when we obey God because his commands are motivated by his love for us.**

GO FOR THE GOAL!

- **TOPIC:** *Perseverance*
- **SCRIPTURE:** *Philippians 3:12-14*
- **SYNOPSIS:** *Group members will work in teams to reach a goal, then discuss not giving up on God's goals for their lives.*
- **BEHIND THE SCENES:** *Write "GOAL" on a sheet of newsprint for each team and tape the sheets to the ceiling. Pour washable paint into a pie pan. You'll also need a bucket of water, soap, paper towels, Bibles, and markers. Let your group know in advance that they'll need to wear old clothes to this meeting.*

 **ACTION!**

Form teams of no more than four. Have each person dip a palm in the paint. Point to the newsprint on the ceiling and say: **Work together so that each team member reaches the "goal" and puts his or her hand print on it. You may not use any furniture to help you reach your goal. Keep your painted hand clenched so you don't get paint on anyone or anything. Go!**

After everyone has reached the goal, have kids use the soap, water, and paper towels to clean their hands (and anything else that inadvertently got painted).

 **CLOSE UP!** Tell the teams to read Philippians 3:12-14 then discuss the following questions. After each question, have team members take turns sharing their team's answers.

Ask: **What challenges did you face in reaching the goal? Why was it easier for some people to reach the goal than others? What are some goals God has for our lives? Do you think God's goals are easier for some people than they are for others? Why or why not? What are some challenges that make you feel like giving up on God's goals for you? What role did your teammates play in helping you reach the goal on the ceiling? How can we support one another in reaching God's goals for our lives? What are some practical ways you could work toward God's goals this week?**

It's a Wrap! Remove the newsprint from the ceiling. Hand out markers. Have kids write their names on their own hand prints. Under their names have them write one goal they'll reach for and not give up on this week.

Have kids tear out and take home their hand prints to remind them to reach for their goals. Close by having kids read their goals aloud. Then pray for your kids by name, asking God to help the kids persevere until their goals are attained.

WHY IN THE WORLD?

- **TOPIC:** *Purpose*
- **SCRIPTURE:** *Ephesians 5:15-17*
- **SYNOPSIS:** *Group members will ask "why?" to help each other determine a purpose in life.*
- **BEHIND THE SCENES:** *You'll need a Bible.*

 **ACTION!**

Form pairs and have partners number off. Have all the ones tell their partners why they think God created them. After they share, have the twos ask "why?" Continue this process until the ones can't think of anything else to say.

Then have partners exchange roles.

CLOSE UP!

Have pairs form groups of four. In their groups, have kids respond to these questions. Ask: **What did you learn about yourself in this experience? about your partner? What discoveries did you make about God? Why is it so hard for people to discover God's purpose for them? How can a process like this help you discover more about why God created you? Based on this experience, what do you think is God's purpose for you?**

It's a Wrap! Read aloud Ephesians 5:15-17. Say: **God wants us to live purposeful lives. Remembering that God had a purpose when he created us can help us make better choices in life. Let's ask God to help us discover why he created us as we go through every day.**

Have kids rejoin their original partners and share with each other one discovery from this session that they'll take with them into the future. Then have pairs pray together for God's help in discovering the full breadth of his purpose for them.

WHO AM I?

- **TOPIC:** *Self-Identity*
- **SCRIPTURE:** *Romans 8:14-16*
- **SYNOPSIS:** *Group members will play a game similar to Twenty Questions and discover who they are in Christ.*
- **BEHIND THE SCENES:** *You'll need to prepare a list of five to 10 famous people with five identifying clues for each person. For example, "George Washington—honesty, revolution, cherry tree, president, dollar bill" or "Michael Jordan—basketball, Nike, Chicago Bulls, baseball, commercials." Also include on your list some of the group members.*

   You'll also need paper, pencils, and Bibles.

CTION! Say: **We're going to play a game similar to Twenty Questions. I'll give you clues that identify a familiar person. After each clue, I'll ask, "Who am I?" to give you a chance to guess the identity of the person. The first one to guess the identity of the person will receive a point.**

Start the game and continue playing until kids have guessed the identity of all the people on your list. The kid with the most points is the winner!

 **CLOSE UP!** Congratulate the winner. Ask: **How hard or easy was it to guess the identity of the person? Why do we usually identify people by their looks or by what they do? Do you think God identifies people that way? Why or why not?**

Say: **Let's look at the way God recognizes who we are.**

Form groups of three or four. Have groups read Romans 8:14-16 and discuss the following questions: **What makes us afraid of God sometimes? Do you think we should be afraid? Why or why not? Based on this passage, do you think God wants us to be afraid of him or glad that we're his children? Explain. What are some things a good father does for his children? How does it feel to know that you have the best father ever—God?**

After groups discuss each question, have each small group report it's responses to the whole group.

It's a Wrap! Distribute paper and a pencil to each person. Have each kid write a letter to God reflecting his or her reactions to the Bible passage. For example, a student might write, "Dear God, thank you for letting me be your child and for letting me call you Father" and so on.

When kids have finished, encourage them to keep their letters in their Bibles to read whenever they feel lost or aren't really sure who they are.

CLEANSED

- **TOPIC:** *Sin and forgiveness*
- **SCRIPTURE:** *1 John 1:7*
- **SYNOPSIS:** *Group members will build a sand sculpture to represent sin then wash it away as a symbol of God's forgiveness.*
- **BEHIND THE SCENES:** *You'll need sand, a small tub, a pitcher of water, and a Bible.*

Action! Place the sand in a tub and mix in enough water to make the sand cohesive. Have kids work together to build a sand sculpture that represents sin. (If you have a large group, form groups and provide a tub of sand for each group.) For example, kids might sculpt a skull and crossbones or an abstract representation. Allow kids five minutes to work as they talk about sins that are common today.

After five minutes, read 1 John 1:7 aloud. As you read, slowly pour water over the sculpture to dissolve it.

 **CLOSE UP!** ♦ Ask: **How did your "sin sculpture" react to water? How is this experience like what happens when God forgives us? when we forgive each other? when we forgive ourselves? How do you feel knowing that God wants to "wash away" all of your sins? What keeps people from asking for God's forgiveness?**

It's a Wrap! ♦ Have kids close their eyes. Say: **Some of you may have sins that you need to confess to God to receive his forgiveness. Take some time in silent prayer now to do that.**

After one or two minutes of silence, close the prayer and thank God for Jesus who makes forgiveness possible.

WAITING...

- **TOPIC:** *Spiritual growth*
- **SCRIPTURE:** *Colossians 1:9-14*
- **SYNOPSIS:** *Group members will learn that spiritual growth takes effort.*
- **BEHIND THE SCENES:** *You'll need snacks, equipment for playing your group's favorite games, and Bibles. Hide the snacks and equipment before the devotion begins.*

 **ACTION!** Have kids sit in a circle.

Say: **Today we have some wonderful plans for our time together. We have some great snacks to enjoy, and we're going to play some of your favorite games.**

After speaking, sit quietly. Kids may become uncomfortable waiting for you to act and may ask when all the fun is going to begin. Simply deflect their questions by reaffirming how wonderful the snacks and games will be.

 **CLOSE UP!** After a few minutes of waiting, form groups of no more than four. Have groups discuss the following questions then share their answers with the class. Ask: **What was it like to sit around wait-**

ing for the food and games to appear? How is that like the way some people live out their faith? What will it take to get the snacks and play the games? What does it take to grow in our relationship with God?

Have someone read aloud Colossians 1:9-14. Then have kids call out ways they can grow spiritually. For example, kids might say, "Read the Bible," "Share faith struggles with friends," or "Pray." Form pairs and have kids take turns telling their partners one way they can grow spiritually using some of the ideas the group named.

It's a Wrap! Have kids collect the snacks and game supplies. Then say: **Just as we can take action to make a fun time happen, we can take action to make spiritual growth happen.**

Have kids find new partners and commit to one or two specific ways they'll work to grow spiritually in the coming weeks. Then close with a prayer, asking God to help your kids find a deeper understanding of what it means to be a Christian.

STRESSED OUT

- **TOPIC:** *Stress*
- **SCRIPTURE:** *Philippians 4:6-7*
- **SYNOPSIS:** *Group members will smash a bag of potato chips and learn that God wants them to depend on him to deal with their stress.*
- **BEHIND THE SCENES:** *You'll need two large bags of potato chips, a bowl, and a Bible.*

 **ACTION!** Sit with kids in a circle. Tell kids to think about something that causes them a lot of stress. Then pass around one bag of potato chips. Have kids name their stressors then squeeze, pound, or twist the bag. Encourage kids not to break open the bag.

 **CLOSE UP!** When the bag returns to you, open it and pour the contents into a bowl. Ask: **Which do you prefer— chips like this or unbroken chips? Why? How are the effects of stress on us similar to or different from what happened to these potato chips?**

Read aloud Philippians 4:6-7. Ask: **What does God want us to do when we're feeling stressed out? How easy or difficult is it for you to do**

what this verse says? How can we let the peace of God reign in our hearts?

It's a Wrap! ◆ Say: **Let's pray for each other and ask God to help us be at peace with the things that are stressing us out.**

Going around the circle, have kids pray about the stressor that was mentioned by the person on their right. After the prayer, open the second bag of potato chips and add it to the bowl. Then pass the chips around for the kids to enjoy. Say: **With God's help, we can turn our "stress" into "strength."**

BELIEVE IT OR NOT!

- **TOPIC:** *Unbelief*
- **SCRIPTURE:** *Galatians 1:6-11*
- **SYNOPSIS:** *Group members will have to decide what to believe and what not to believe.*
- **BEHIND THE SCENES:** *You'll need to check out a copy of* Ripley's Believe It or Not! *from your local library. Mark one short entry for each group member. You'll also need Bibles.*

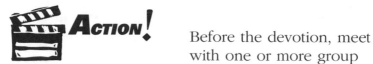 **ACTION!** Before the devotion, meet with one or more group members and give them a false "believe it or not" story they can practice saying convincingly in their own words. When the session begins, pass around the *Ripley's Believe It or Not!* book and have each kid choose one story to learn and convey to the rest of the group.

When everyone has learned a story, gather everyone in a circle and say: **Let's take turns describing our amazing events or facts to the whole group in our own words. But beware! There is a deceiver in your midst who has a "fake" story. When everyone has shared, we'll see if we can find the deceiver.**

Go around the circle, giving each person about 30 seconds to describe his or her Ripley's entry. Then ask kids to vote on who they think is the deceiver. Award the winners with a round of applause.

 **CLOSE UP!** Ask: **Was it hard for you to figure out who was trying to deceive you? Why or why not?**

Distribute Bibles and have everyone follow along as you read Galatians 1:6-11 aloud. Ask: **Regarding spiritual truth, how hard or easy is it for you to see through deception? When have you been tempted not to believe an essential truth of the Bible? What caused you to doubt? How do circumstances sometimes work against our belief in God and our trust in his Word? How can we continue to believe**

during those "doubting" times? Why is it important that we not give in to unbelief?

It's a Wrap! Tell kids you're going to pass around a copy of "Jehovah's Believe It or Not." As kids pass around a copy of the Bible, have them each share one of their most cherished Bible-based beliefs, or one of the toughest doubts they've encountered in their walk with God.

SCARED INTO IT?

- **TOPIC:** *Wisdom*
- **SCRIPTURE:** *Psalm 111:10*
- **SYNOPSIS:** *Group members will list ways to be wise and explore what it means to fear God.*
- **BEHIND THE SCENES:** *You'll need paper slips, pencils, a hat, and a Bible.*

 **ACTION!** Give each person two paper slips and a pencil. Have kids write on one of their slips the #1 way to get wisdom. After kids have finished, have them fold their slips

and put them into the hat. Once you've collected all the slips, read them aloud one at a time. Afterward, have kids vote on the idea they liked best.

Read aloud Psalm 111:10. Ask: **Why does God say that the beginning of wisdom is to fear him? According to this verse, does God want us to be afraid of him? Why or why not? What does it mean to "fear God" (NIV)? How can this kind of fear lead to wisdom?**

 **CLOSE UP!** Have kids write on their remaining slips one way they can grow in wisdom. Have kids form trios and tell their group members what they wrote. In their trios, have kids respond to these questions: **Why is wisdom important? According to the verse we read, is it possible to be wise and not know God? Why or why not? How will the action you've chosen help you gain wisdom in the future?**

It's a Wrap! Have trio partners exchange their paper slips and pray together asking God to help their partners grow in wisdom this week. Encourage kids to call each other during the coming week to see how they're doing with their commitment.

Looking at Our Faith

Scene 2:
Looking at
Our World

EYE TO EYE

- **TOPIC:** *Acceptance*
- **SCRIPTURE:** *Romans 15:1-7*
- **SYNOPSIS:** *Group members will experience being avoided and accepted, then discuss how to accept others as Christ accepts them.*
- **BEHIND THE SCENES:** *You'll need one Bible for every five kids.*

**ACTION!** Form groups of five. Say:
Form a circle then choose one person to stand in the center. If you're the center person, your goal is to get each of your group members to make eye contact with you. If you're part of the circle, your goal is to avoid eye contact with the center person without closing your eyes. After your center person has tried to make eye contact with each person in your group, everyone huddle together and give the center person a group hug. Go!

Have groups repeat the activity until everyone has had a turn in the middle.

**CLOSE UP!** Have kids number off within their groups. Say:
Discuss the next few questions in your

groups. After each question, I'll call out a number from one to five. The person in your group whose number I call out will be responsible for sharing your group's answer.

Ask: **How did you feel when no one in your group would look at you? How did it feel to get a group hug? What are some ways people reject others in real life? What's your reaction when others reject you? Have you ever rejected someone else? What made you do it? Why is it sometimes easier to reject than to accept?**

Hand out Bibles and have one person in each group read Romans 15:1-7 aloud. Ask: **What stands out most to you from this passage? How does knowing that Christ accepts you impact you? What do you need from this group to feel truly accepted? What can you do to help others in this group feel accepted?**

It's a Wrap!

Say: **One way we can accept others is to recognize their positive qualities. Take a minute and think of one positive quality you see in each of the people in your group.** Give kids a minute to think, have groups form circles again, then say: **Now choose one person to stand in the middle. This time, make eye contact with the center person and say the positive quality you appreciate about that person. Be sure everyone gets a turn in the center.**

THE BATTLE IS TOUGH!

- **TOPIC:** *Being a Christian in a non-Christian world*
- **SCRIPTURE:** *1 John 2:15-17*
- **SYNOPSIS:** *Group members will hear two different rhythms and try to discern which one they should march to.*
- **BEHIND THE SCENES:** *You'll need Bibles, a Walkman, a cassette player, and two cassette tapes with different songs on them.*

 **ACTION!** Put the tape with the faster tempo in the cassette player and place the tape with the slower tempo in the Walkman.

Say: **We're going to try a little experiment. I'm going to play a song on the cassette player. While the song is playing, I'm going to clap out a rhythm that doesn't match the song. I want you to try to march in place to the rhythm I create. Then, when I stop, see if you can keep marching to the rhythm that I've set until I begin to clap it out again.**

Put on the Walkman's headphones. Start both cassette players and clap out the rhythm to the song on your Walkman. Stop clapping every few seconds to see if kids can keep marching at the pace you've set.

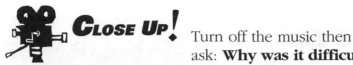

CLOSE UP! Turn off the music then ask: **Why was it difficult to march to the rhythm I set? Were you able to keep my tempo even when I stopped clapping? Explain. Was it more difficult to keep the beat in the beginning or near the end? Why?**

Read 1 John 2:15-17 aloud. Ask: **How is being a Christian in a non-Christian world like marching to a beat that doesn't agree with the song everyone else is listening to?**

It's a Wrap! Play the song you were listening to on the cassette player loud enough so everyone can hear it. Have kids form pairs and discuss these questions with their partners: **What things in daily life cause you to "lose the rhythm" of your Christian walk? How can you keep marching to Christ's beat no matter what the rest of the world is doing? How can we help each other this week to live out our faith more boldly?**

DO YOU LOVE YOUR NEIGHBOR?

- **TOPIC:** *Biblical principles in relationships*
- **SCRIPTURE:** *Matthew 22:37-39*
- **SYNOPSIS:** *Group members will discuss how to fulfill Christ's command to love others.*
- **BEHIND THE SCENES:** *You'll need Bibles, paper, and pencils.*

 **ACTION!** Tell the kids to each grab a chair and form a circle. Stand in the center of the circle and say: **I am the Questioner. In a moment, I'll go up to a person and ask, "Do you love your neighbor?" That person may respond by saying yes or no. If the answer is no, the people on either side of that person will have to exchange seats. However, during the exchange, I'll try to steal one of the seats! If I succeed, then the person left standing will take over as the Questioner.**

If I ask, "Do you love your neighbor?" and the person says yes, then I'll ask "Why do you love your neighbor?" The person will have to respond by saying, "I love my neighbor because he (or she) **is . . ." and adding on a fact about that person. For example, " . . . because he is wearing a white T-shirt" or " . . . because she owns a CD Walkman."**

After the person speaks, each person in the room for whom that fact is true must get up and find a new seat. For example, if the person says she loves her neighbor because he is wearing a white T-shirt, then everyone wearing a white T-shirt must get up and find a new seat. Once again, whoever is left standing becomes the new Questioner.

 **CLOSE UP!** After playing several rounds of the game, form groups of three or four and ask group members to read Matthew 22:37-39. Ask the groups to discuss the following questions and be prepared to share their answers with the whole group. Ask: **How do you feel when others treat you wrong? when you treat others wrong? when you treat yourself wrong? According to these verses, how does loving God help us to love ourselves and others? Why is love the most important aspect of all our relationships? What are some ways you can make love a more prominent focus of your relationships with your friends? with your family? with yourself?**

 **It's a Wrap!** Distribute paper and pencils and have kids write something they will do for someone they love this week. Tell them to tape the papers to their bathroom mirrors so they'll remember to follow

through, and so they can pray for those people.

Close by singing "They Will Know We Are Christians by Our Love" or a similar song.

JOINED TOGETHER

- ● **TOPIC:** *The body of Christ*
- ● **SCRIPTURE:** *Ephesians 2:20-21; 4:16*
- ● **SYNOPSIS:** *Group members will build two houses—one that's unsteady and one that's held together by Christ.*
- ● **BEHIND THE SCENES:** *You'll need 3×5 cards, pencils, glue, and Bibles.*

 **ACTION!** Give each person four 3×5 cards. Form groups of four. Have each group build the tallest and sturdiest card house that they can in two minutes.

After two minutes, call time. Then ask: **Were you successful in your attempt to build a sturdy card house? What made it frustrating? What was important in building a tall and sturdy house? How is your card house like living without Christ?**

CLOSE UP!

Have each group read Ephesians 2:20-21 then discuss these questions: **What foundation did the apostles and the prophets give to the building? Why is Jesus Christ the strongest stone in the building? How does Christ join the building together?** Have a volunteer from each group share his or her group's discoveries with the rest of the class.

Next, have each group read Ephesians 4:16. Ask: **How can the building of Christ be strengthened?** Have each person take another four 3×5 cards and a pencil. Have kids write their names on one of their cards and the names of his or her group members on the other three cards. Then have kids write a talent, gift, or ability each person has that might contribute to making the "whole body grow and be strong with love." For example, someone might write, "Chris, a strong encourager" or "Kari, a great leader." Have the kids read what they've written to their group members.

It's a Wrap!

Gather each group's cards. Read Ephesians 4:16 aloud. Then hold up the cards and the glue and say: **Each of you has talents and abilities that can help the church grow and be strong, but Christ is the one that glues us all together.**

Work together to build another card house. This time fold the edges of the cards and glue them together. As you glue the cards together, read what's written on them.

Keep the card house on display in your group's room. As new kids join your group, fill out cards for them and add them to the house.

LOOK WHO'S TALKING

- **TOPIC:** *Communication*
- **SCRIPTURE:** *Ephesians 4:29*
- **SYNOPSIS:** *Group members will try to communicate in unusual ways and learn that there's more to talking than just words.*
- **BEHIND THE SCENES:** *You'll need Bibles.*

ACTION! Form two groups and give each group a separate "important message" that they'll communicate to the other group. For example, the message might be "Don't use words to hurt people" or "A kind word is powerful medicine for the heart."

Here's the catch: Tell each group they can communicate using only facial expressions and one other body part, such as a leg or an elbow. They may not use their voices in any way other than grunting.

Give each group a minute to decide how its members will each convey the message. Then have each group member find a partner from the other group and let kids take turns trying to con-

vey their assigned message. Allow a few minutes
for the attempt.

CLOSE UP!

After the experience, gather
everyone together and ask:
**What was your reaction to trying to communicate
in this way? Why was it so hard to get even a sim-
ple message across? How did you try to overcome
the language limitation? How was the experience
like what happens in real life when two people
misunderstand each other? When have you felt
like somebody failed to understand what you
were saying? When have you failed to understand
what someone else was trying to tell you? What
did you do in those situations to work through
the communication barrier?**

Have a volunteer read Ephesians 4:29 aloud.
Then ask: **How can focusing on the other person's needs help make communication clear-
er? Why is it hard for us to do what this verse
says? What's the payoff for us if we do commit
ourselves to "other-centered" communication?
What's one way you can start that commitment this week?**

It's a Wrap!

Have kids rejoin their partners and tell them one way
they are good communicators. Then have pairs
pray together, asking God to give them the grace
to become "other-centered" communicators.

Looking at Our World

SCARY SCULPTING

- **TOPIC:** *Death*
- **SCRIPTURE:** *1 Corinthians 15:20-26*
- **SYNOPSIS:** *In considering their own deaths, group members will realize that death itself will one day cease to exist.*
- **BEHIND THE SCENES:** *You'll need Bibles and pencils. You'll also need two coin-sized circles of gray or silver construction paper for each person.*

 **ACTION!** Have kids form a circle, then say: **As we go around the circle, I want you to pose in a position that shows how you think you might die. Be sure to include what you think your facial expression will be in the last moments—and be ready to explain the circumstances of your "death" in detail.**

Allow kids a few minutes to consider how they might die. Then go around the circle and have kids demonstrate their "death sculptures." As each kid does his or her sculpture, have the rest of the group try to guess the circumstances being depicted.

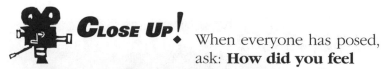 **CLOSE UP!** When everyone has posed, ask: **How did you feel when you had to imagine your own death? Why do we so rarely talk about something so absolutely certain—our own approaching deaths? What's the scariest thing for you about contemplating your death? about contemplating the death of people you love?**

It's a Wrap! Have kids read 1 Corinthians 15:20-26 silently. Ask for volunteers to summarize the basic theme of the passage. Then display your construction paper "coins" and say: **In the old days, coins were placed on a dead person's eyelids to keep them closed.**

Distribute pencils and coins. On one side of their coins, have kids write the thing that scares them most about death. On the other side of their coins, ask kids to write this short verse: "The last enemy to be destroyed will be death" (1 Corinthians 15:26). Ask: **What's your greatest fear about death? How would believing the verse written on your coin change your perspective on death?**

Say: **When we think about our coming deaths, it's good to remember both sides of the coin: Death may be our enemy, but Jesus has defeated it on our behalf.**

LET'S GIVE THEM A HAND

- **TOPIC:** Encouraging others
- **SCRIPTURE:** Isaiah 41:13
- **SYNOPSIS:** Group members will discover that giving encouragement is natural because we receive encouragement from God.
- **BEHIND THE SCENES:** You'll need a Bible and a blindfold for every two people. Clear the room of any obstacles that might trip or injure the blindfolded group members.

 **ACTION!** Form pairs and have one partner put a blindfold over the other partner's eyes. After all blindfolds are in place, count to 10 while the "sighted" partners spin the "blinded" partners as fast as they can.

When you've finished counting, say: **I want the sighted partners to quietly move to the edges of the room and remain perfectly quiet. Then I want the blinded partners to "go on a quest" to find their partners. Walk carefully and slowly and keep talking so the other blinded people know where you are. Once you find your partner, you can remove your blindfold.**

After kids have been searching for their partners for a few minutes, say to the sighted partners: **Now I want you to call out to your partner and guide him or her to you using only your voice.**

Continue the activity until all the pairs are

together, then have the blinded partners remove
their blindfolds.

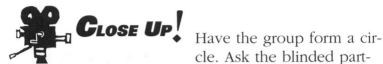 **CLOSE UP!** Have the group form a cir-
cle. Ask the blinded part-
ners: **How did you feel as you were trying to
find your partner without any help? How is
that like how it feels sometimes to try to find
encouragement when you feel down?**

Ask the sighted partners: **How did you feel
watching your partners try to find you without being able to help? How did you feel when
you could finally call to them? How is that like
how it feels to try to encourage your friends
when they're down?**

Ask everyone: **How is this experience similar
to how it feels to try to receive encouragement
from God? How is it similar to the way God
might feel as he's trying to encourage you?
What do we have to do before God can encourage us? How does receiving God's encouragement help us to encourage others?**

It's a Wrap! Read Isaiah 41:13 aloud.
Then say: **Let's encourage
each other the way God encourages us.**

Have kids turn to the person on their right, hold
right hands, and give a word of encouragement to
each other by completing this statement: "I am
thankful to God for you because..." For example,

kids might say, "I am thankful to God for you because you're always kind to me" or "I'm thankful to God for you because you always help others."

THIS IS WAR!

- **TOPIC:** *Enemies*
- **SCRIPTURE:** *Luke 6:27-36*
- **SYNOPSIS:** *Group members will experience the difficult task of "turning the other cheek" as they explore how to respond to enemies.*
- **BEHIND THE SCENES:** *Let your group know in advance that they'll need to wear old clothes to this meeting. You'll need a canister full of flour, paper towels for cleanup, Bibles, and a batch of cookies.*

 **ACTION!** Form two teams. Have each team come up with a team name and three reasons why they're enemies with the other team. For example, a team might say, "We don't like the other team because they secretly love peanut butter and mosquito sandwiches."

Then give one team the canister of flour. Have each kid on this team flick or toss a small amount of flour in a rival team member's face. Tell the team members who are getting flour tossed in their faces to stand still and just be patient.

After each person on the flour-throwing team has had a turn, say: **Now, the second team will have a chance to . . . get hit again with flour.**

Have the first team repeat tossing flour on the second team. Kids on the second team may try to retaliate, but encourage them to wait.

When the second round of flour tossing is over, tell everyone the activity is over. You'll hear plenty of grumbles from the second team, but that's OK.

 **CLOSE UP!** Form groups consisting of members from both teams. Then have kids discuss the following questions in their groups before sharing their answers with the whole group. Ask: **What was it like to be on the throwing end of this flour-tossing contest? What was it like to be on the receiving end?**

Have groups read Luke 6:27-36. Then have them discuss these questions: **What does this passage tell us about enemies? How was our activity an example of living out this message? What's different about dealing with enemies in everyday life? What are ways people can stop being enemies?**

Say: **The Bible calls for us to love our enemies—something that's easier said than done.**

Have kids tell of experiences where they did or did not respond in a loving way to "enemies." Then have kids form pairs and take turns praying for each other to follow the biblical teaching about dealing with enemies.

It's a Wrap! Have kids share a batch of cookies to celebrate the fact that they aren't enemies. Have the flour-tossing team members serve the rival team's members (without throwing any of the cookies).

Close by having kids sing a song such as "They Will Know We Are Christians by Our Love."

FAMILY MATTERS

- **TOPIC:** *Family*
- **SCRIPTURE:** *Matthew 5:14-16*
- **SYNOPSIS:** *Group members will use modeling clay to see how they influence their families.*
- **BEHIND THE SCENES:** *You'll need several different colors of modeling clay and a Bible.*

 **ACTION!** Give each person a small lump of clay from each color. Have kids shape a clay person to represent each member of their family, including themselves. After they've finished, read aloud these situations and have kids follow the directions in parentheses:

Read: **Your brother or sister is mad because your parents won't let you have a party while they're out of town. He or she suggests that you**

have the party anyway. You say "no" and don't let it happen. (Press the clay figure of yourself against the sibling figure and leave it there.)

Read: **Your mom is sad because a good friend died. You encourage your mom by telling her that her friend believed in Jesus and went to heaven. (Remove the sibling figure and press the clay figure of yourself against your parent figure and leave it.)**

Read: **Your other family members notice how you're always encouraging others and helping people with their problems. (Press the sibling figure against the figures of the parent and yourself and leave it.)**

 **CLOSE UP!** Ask: **What happened to the colors of your clay family during this experience? How did the clay figure of yourself change the other figures in your clay family? How has God used you to change "people" in your family?**

Read Matthew 5:14-16 aloud. Then ask: **How can you impact your family for the better?**

Say: **Use your clay to create a symbol that represents something good about your family. For example, you may make a big heart because your family is loving or a tennis racket because your family is athletic.**

It's a Wrap! Form a circle. One at a time, have kids show their clay creations and say, "I'm thankful for my family because we're..."

Close with prayer asking God to use kids to influence their families for God.

FRUITY FRIENDS

- **TOPIC:** *Friends*
- **SCRIPTURE:** *John 15:12-17 and Galatians 5:22-23*
- **SYNOPSIS:** *Group members will examine the important qualities of being a friend.*
- **BEHIND THE SCENES:** *Fill a basket with fruit then label each piece of fruit with a different "fruit of the Spirit" listed in Galatians 5:22-23. You'll also need a Bible.*

 **Action!** Form groups of four. Bring out the basket of labeled fruit and have each group select one piece of fruit. In their groups, have kids try to come up with a "Top 10 List" for how this fruit of the spirit would enhance a friendship.

When groups have finished, have each group share its "Top 10 List." For every enhancement a group lists, ask volunteers to share how they've experienced that situation in their own friendships.

 **CLOSE UP!** After the discussion, have each group read together John 15:12-17 and discuss these questions: **What do you think Jesus means when he says, "The greatest love a person can show is to die for his friends"? What's the greatest sacrifice a friend has made for you? What's the most sacrificial thing you've done for a friend? What's the most hurtful thing a friend can do to you? How do you feel about your friendship with Jesus? Are you willing to sacrifice for him? Why or why not?**

It's a Wrap! Have the small groups return to the large group and sit in a circle. Collect the pieces of fruit in the basket, then say: **I'd like to pass the basket one more time. This time, please choose a "fruit of the Spirit" that reflects a quality that you see in the person on your right. Tell how you see that "fruit" in action in that person's life. When you're finished, place the piece of fruit back into the basket and pass it to the next person.**

When kids have finished, have them share the basket of fruit as a celebration of their friendship. If your group is large, have extra fruit on hand.

TEARS CAN HELP

- **TOPIC:** *Grief*
- **SCRIPTURE:** *Revelation 21:1-4*
- **SYNOPSIS:** *Group members will experience the hindrance of tears but will also learn of their healing potential.*
- **BEHIND THE SCENES:** *You'll need two or three bottles of saline solution, and a box of tissues. Also, write or print out the Bible passage with super-small lettering. Make a copy of the passage for each person and fold each copy in half.*

ACTION! Distribute copies of the Scripture passage and ask kids not to unfold the papers until you tell them to. Have everyone gather in a circle then say: **In a moment, we're going to unfold our papers and read in unison the Bible passage printed there. But first, let's lubricate our eyes so we can read better.**

Pass the bottles of saline solution around and have kids put a few drops in their eyes. Before kids can clear their eyes, tell them to begin reading. After the first read through, have group members read the Scripture a few more times with you.

CLOSE UP! Ask: **What was it like to read this wonderful, positive message about grief? How was reading the passage with tears in our eyes like trying to get on with life when you're grieving? What kinds of situations in life require us to keep going in spite of our tears? How can those situations be good for us? How can they be bad for us?**

Read Revelation 21:1-4 aloud again. Then say: **God has promised to wipe away our tears someday because he's going to wipe away all pain, and even death itself. But in the meantime, we often must look at life through our tears. Crying is a healthy, healing part of dealing with pain.**

It's a Wrap! Tell kids you're going to pass a box of tissues around the circle while they sit in silence. Invite kids to take a tissue only if they promise to share with a parent or friend this week a grief that burdens them.

Close by saying: **Keep your tissue in your Bible as a reminder to share your grief with the people who love you.**

MAKING A DIFFERENCE

- **TOPIC:** *Impacting others*
- **SCRIPTURE:** *Acts 1:8*
- **SYNOPSIS:** *Group members will "map out" their relationships and discuss the difference they're making in people's lives.*
- **BEHIND THE SCENES:** *You'll need a detailed map of your community, tape, pushpins, index cards, and a Bible. Tape the map to a bulletin board.*

 **ACTION!** Gather kids around the map of your community. Ask kids to think about the close relationships they have with people in your community, including family and friends.

Read Acts 1:8 aloud. Then say: **God has placed you in this community for a reason. God has placed people in your life so that you can love them and help them grow closer to God. Let's take a look at all the people we know who we can reach out to.** Have kids stick pushpins in the areas where the people they have thought of live.

 **CLOSE UP!** Say: **Look at all the people we know!** Ask: **Have you ever thought of these people in terms of**

their need for God's love? Why or why not? What obstacles keep you from telling them about God's love? What obstacles keep you from doing something for them that will show God's love? What can you do to impact one of these people for God this week?

It's a Wrap! Have each kid remove the pushpins he or she placed on the map. Tell each kid to write the names he or she thought of on an index card. Then have kids take their cards home to hang on a wall or bulletin board as reminders of the people they are close to. Encourage kids to focus on making an impact for God in these people's lives over the next several months.

LEARNING WITH STYLE

- **TOPIC:** *Learning*
- **SCRIPTURE:** *Proverbs 4:5-9*
- **SYNOPSIS:** *Group members will discover the value of learning as they're taught how to solve a puzzle.*
- **BEHIND THE SCENES:** *You'll need a "mind boggler" puzzle such as a Rubik's Cube, instructions on how to solve the puzzle, illustrations or photographs of someone solving the puzzle, and Bibles.*

 **ACTION!** Have kids gather around as you explain that you're going to teach them how to solve a difficult puzzle.

Begin by simply reading the instructions on solving the puzzle (without letting kids handle the puzzle). Then ask: **OK, who knows how to solve the puzzle?** If all the group members respond positively, have each of them try to solve the puzzle (without looking at the instructions).

If not all the kids answer yes, let kids read the solution and look at the pictures of someone solving the puzzle. Again ask if anyone knows how to solve the puzzle. If all say yes, have them begin taking turns solving the puzzle.

If not all the kids say yes, show them how to solve the puzzle. Then undo the puzzle and work with the kids to help them come up with the solution for themselves.

 **CLOSE UP!** Once the puzzle is solved, have kids form groups of no more than four to discuss the following questions: **What did it take for you to learn how to solve this puzzle? How many types of learning were used in this activity?**

Read Proverbs 4:5-9 aloud and ask: **What does this passage tell us about the value of learning? How can that be applied to our puzzle solving? to school? to faith? to other aspects of life?**

Have kids tell about times they've had difficulty learning a concept or activity. Then have volunteers share ideas for making learning more fun. Encourage kids to practice these ideas as they pursue knowledge in all areas of life, especially their faith.

 **It's a Wrap!** Form a circle, and have kids offer one-sentence prayers for the persons on their right. Ask each kid to thank God for a unique quality that person has that makes him or her an "essential puzzle piece" for the youth group.

GIMME

- **TOPIC:** *Money*
- **SCRIPTURE:** *1 Timothy 6:6-11*
- **SYNOPSIS:** *Group members will learn that godliness is more valuable than money.*
- **BEHIND THE SCENES:** *You'll need a large supply of quarters, a few dollar bills, a bunch of paper slips with 1 Timothy 6:6-11 written on them, and Bibles.*

ACTION! Say: **To begin our devotion, I'd like to give each person here a gift. You can choose either**

money or a few good words of advice.

Hand 50 cents to the kids who choose money and give the slips of paper to the kids who choose advice.

When everyone has chosen, ask: **Was it easy to make your choice? Why or why not? Why did you choose the item you did? How confident are you that your chosen item is worth the most?**

Go around the room and give a dollar bill to each person who chose the advice. Explain that the advice they chose is worth much more than the money and that you wanted to help them realize this by giving them a token. (If no one chose the advice, explain what would have happened.)

CLOSE UP! Form groups of no more than four. Have kids read 1 Timothy 6:6-11 then discuss the following questions before sharing their group's responses.

Ask: **What does this passage tell us about the value of godliness versus money? How did you feel if you chose the advice then were given more money than the other kids? How did you feel if you chose the money then watched the other kids get more money than you? How is this experience like the message of this passage?**

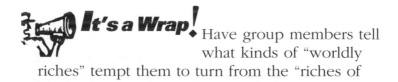

It's a Wrap! Have group members tell what kinds of "worldly riches" tempt them to turn from the "riches of faith." Kids might suggest things such as video games, a new car, clothes, or movies. Then have kids choose one of the traits listed in 1 Timothy 6:11 that they want to pursue instead.

Form trios and have kids pray that their partners will pursue traits of godliness rather than be driven by the pursuit of worldly riches.

GOD IN A BOX?

- **TOPIC:** *Other religions*
- **SCRIPTURE:** *Romans 2:11-16*
- **SYNOPSIS:** *Group members will share what they know about God and discover that they have something in common with people from other Christian denominations or groups.*
- **BEHIND THE SCENES:** *You'll need a poster board sign with the word "God" written on it in large letters. You'll also need a shoe box, 3×5 cards, tape, pencils, and Bibles.*

 **ACTION!**
Place a shoe box on a table. Tape the poster board sign to the wall behind the shoe box.

Give each kid several 3×5 cards and a pencil. Say: **I'm going to give you five minutes to jot down everything you know—or believe—about**

God. Write one thing on each card.

For example, kids could write biblical attributes of God, events attributed to God, or any thoughts or theories they have about God's true nature. Have kids toss the completed cards into the shoe box.

CLOSE UP! When everyone has finished, pull the cards out of the box and hold them up in one hand. In the other hand, hold up the "God" poster board sign. Say: **Let's say this sign represents God. If that's so, then how much of "God" do you think all these cards explain? Are these two things the same—our thoughts about God and God himself? Why or why not? Do you think it's possible to understand God the way he understands us? Why or why not?**

Ask kids to think about their attitudes toward people in other Christian denominations as you read Romans 2:11-16 aloud. Say: **We've been given the essential truth about God and salvation, but there is still no one who knows everything about God. God is infinite, and our theologies have limits.**

Ask: **How could knowing that no denomination "has it all" affect your attitude toward different Christian groups?**

It's a Wrap! Ask each kid to take a card from the shoe box, read it, then turn it over. Then have each kid write the name of a person he or she knows who could benefit from the information written on the card. Have kids spend a minute or two in silent prayer asking God for the courage to tell that person about God.

Close by saying: **We're responsible for following and sharing the laws of God. So . . . share what you know—in humility—knowing that you don't know all!**

BUT AREN'T THEY THE ENEMY?

- **TOPIC:** *Prejudice*
- **SCRIPTURE:** *John 10:16*
- **SYNOPSIS:** *Group members will see that Jesus Christ has followers in many races.*
- **BEHIND THE SCENES:** *You'll need safety pins, several colors of paper, and Bibles. You'll also need a picture of Jesus.*

 **ACTION!** Set out three colors of paper and safety pins. Have each kid choose a color and pin one of the colored sheets to his or her clothes. Then have kids form three groups based on their color choice.

Say: **Imagine that you're members of a particular race based on the color you chose. For**

example, if you chose green, you are the Green Race. For the next few minutes, go around the room and try to convince the other "races" that your race is the best. The key is that you have to mention God somewhere in your argument. For example, you could say, "The Purple Race is best because purple is the color of royalty, and God is the king of the universe" or "The Green Race is best because God made grass and trees green." Make your point as clearly as you can.

After five minutes, gather the groups together and ask: **Did you convince anyone that your race was best? Were you convinced by anyone else? Do you think being loud, obnoxious, and hateful helps convince anyone? Do people ever act like this in real life when trying to convince others that their beliefs about races are correct? Explain.**

 **CLOSE UP!** Read John 10:16 and ask: **What did Jesus mean when he said that he had "other sheep that are not in this flock"? Why didn't the Jews believe the gospel was for everyone? Why do some people today believe that their color or cultural perspective is better than others? How would Jesus respond to the prejudice in the world today? How can you follow in his steps?**

Looking at Our World

It's a Wrap! Form trios and have them brainstorm activities that would help them understand or identify with other ethnic groups in their own community. For example, the group might invite kids from an ethnically-diverse church to join them for a volleyball game and Bible study.

Have trios share their ideas with the rest of the group. Then gather kids together and kneel in the middle of the room. As you pass the picture of Jesus around the circle, have kids take turns thanking God that Jesus came for everyone.

PUT IT BACK TOGETHER!

- **TOPIC:** *Restoring broken relationships*
- **SCRIPTURE:** *Ephesians 4:31-32*
- **SYNOPSIS:** *Group members will break a string of beads in order to consider how "scattered" relationships can be restored.*
- **BEHIND THE SCENES:** *You'll need a large string of fake pearls or plastic beads.*

 **Action!** Ask everyone to stand in a tight circle, then display the string of beads. Say: **Imagine this is something**

you all really want. It represents the most important thing in the world to you. It would be very hard to let it go. In fact, once you get your hands on it, you'll do just about anything to keep it. What would that thing be for you? Allow a moment of silence here.

Have everyone take hold of the string or, depending on the size of your group, at least wrap a finger around it. Tell group members they'll have 10 seconds to pull for what they want—the whole string—so no one else can get it.

On "go," stand back and prompt kids by saying: **You want it bad; this is important to you; you'd be hurt and envious if it went to someone else.**

**Close Up!** ♦ When the string breaks, gather the kids together and read Ephesians 4:31-32 aloud. Ask: **How hard or easy was it to generate a sense of bitterness, or anger about something that wasn't actually important to you? How easy or hard is it to have those kinds of feelings when you're trying to hold on to something that's really important to you? How does your desire to hold onto something important—a thing, an attitude, a sense of pride—cause relationships to break up and scatter?**

Say: **Broken relationships can be restored. But it takes a lot of patience and hard work—and, especially, a willingness to forgive.**

Tell students that it's time to put the necklace back together. Here's how: Have kids each pick up one bead and take turns putting the beads back on the string. As each kid restrings a bead, have him or her name one practical action he or she can take to restore a broken relationship.

It's a Wrap! Invite kids to gather the remaining beads from the floor. On one of the beads, ask them to envision the name and face of someone they no longer have a relationship with. While holding their beads, have kids pray silently that they could develop a new sense of forgiveness for that person.

RADICAL INITIATIVE

- **TOPIC:** *Serving Christ*
- **SCRIPTURE:** *Matthew 5:38-42*
- **SYNOPSIS:** *Group members will examine what it means to intentionally serve Christ.*
- **BEHIND THE SCENES:** *You'll need a building block (or small box), a Bible, and a marker for each person.*

 **Action!** Form two teams. Distribute blocks and markers, then say: **In your team, think of as many actions as**

possible that you do automatically—without thinking. For example, you don't have to think about breathing in order to do it. Write each action on one side of a block and build as high a tower as possible. At the end of three minutes, we'll see which team has the highest tower.

After three minutes, determine which team's tower is the highest. Have that team tell all the "automatic" actions it came up with. When that team has finished, have the other team add their ideas.

 **CLOSE UP!** Have kids discuss these questions in their teams: **What do you "automatically" want to do when someone insults you? What about when someone takes something that belongs to you? when someone bullies you? when someone demands something from you?**

Read aloud Matthew 5:38-42. Repeat the questions, this time having the teams answer them according to Jesus' commands. Then ask: **How are the actions listed on your towers different from what it's like for you to serve God?**

 **It's a Wrap!** Have kids take their blocks from their team's towers and write on them one intentional way they will serve Christ this week. As a whole group, build a tower with the revised blocks.

Close by saying: **With God's help, and lots of**

practice, following Jesus' commands can become as automatic as breathing. Let's pray silently for God's power to transform us into people who choose to serve "automatically".

I'VE GOT A SECRET

- **TOPIC:** *Sharing faith*
- **SCRIPTURE:** *2 Timothy 1:7-12*
- **SYNOPSIS:** *Group members will explore God's call to share their faith, and their temptation to hide it.*
- **BEHIND THE SCENES:** *You'll need Bibles, construction paper, scissors, tape, markers, and yarn.*

 **ACTION!** Set out the paper and other materials on a table and invite kids to make cross necklaces. Say: **Make your necklace as "beautiful" as possible—a work of art— because it'll be judged for artistic quality.**

When kids have finished, have them vote on the most beautiful necklace. Then have kids bring their necklaces and leave the room with you. Explain: **You'll each have 10 seconds to reenter the room, hide your necklace, and come back out.**

Once all the necklaces have been hidden, let the group return to the room and hold a contest to see who can find the most necklaces. After a minute, declare a winner.

CLOSE UP!

Gather everyone in a circle and ask: **How would you describe the "beauty" of the gospel to someone who'd never heard it before? How was hiding our cross necklaces like or unlike our unwillingness to tell others about our relationship with Christ?**

Form pairs and have the partners study 2 Timothy 1:7-12 together. Have kids discuss the following questions in their pairs and tell them to be prepared to share their responses: **What situations make you the most unwilling to talk about your faith in Christ? What situations can make it impossible to hide your Christianity?**

Let kids know they can share about a situation that they've actually experienced or one that could happen. After all the pairs have shared, say: **Though the gospel is the beautiful message of forgiveness through Christ, Paul knew that Christians are often tempted to be ashamed of their faith. This is true mainly because sharing our faith makes us "stand out from the crowd"—and separates us from all other philosophies of life.**

It's a Wrap!

Ask: **How would you rate your level of excitement in identifying with Christ? To what extent have you been ashamed of sharing your faith? Why?**

Ask students to return all the cross necklaces to the original owners. Distribute markers and say: **Write your name on your cross if you are willing at this moment to say to Jesus, "Lord, help**

Looking at Our World

me this week not to be ashamed of you or
your message."

BREAKING BREAD TOGETHER

- **TOPIC:** *Unity*
- **SCRIPTURE:** *John 6:35; 1 Corinthians 10:17; and Ephesians 4:2-3*
- **SYNOPSIS:** *Group members will "partake" of Christ and see how they are each a part of Christ's body.*
- **BEHIND THE SCENES:** *You'll need a fresh-baked loaf of bread (preferably still warm), a plate, and a Bible.*

 **ACTION!** Have kids form a circle.
Say: **Imagine that you
haven't eaten for two days. You're not just
hungry, you're starving!**

Place the plate of fresh bread in the center of
the circle. Say: **Now remember, you'll all starve
to death if you don't eat. You've "discovered"
this loaf of bread, but you have to make sure
everyone in the group gets the same amount
of bread. You have no knives or other uten-**

sils. Decide how to divide the bread equally.

Allow three or four minutes for the group to decide and put their plan into action. After the loaf has been divided, ask: **Was it difficult to decide how to divide the loaf? Why or why not? Would it have been more difficult if you'd really been starving? Why or why not? How did it feel once you'd decided how to divide it? How was this experience like building unity in our group?**

CLOSE UP! Form groups of no more than four. Tell groups to read John 6:35 and 1 Corinthians 10:17. Then have kids discuss the following questions in their groups: **What does it mean to be unified in Christ? Should Christians ever have differences of opinion? If so, how should they settle those differences? What can you do to make "Christian unity" more of a reality in our group?**

It's a Wrap! Read Ephesians 4:2-3 aloud. Have the kids join hands while they sing a song that focuses on Christian unity, such as "Bind Us Together."

Looking at Our World

Scene 3:
Looking at Our Special Days

FOREVER CHANGED

- **TOPIC:** *Christmas*
- **SCRIPTURE:** *Luke 2:1-21 and Matthew 2:1-12*
- **SYNOPSIS:** *Group members will race to a goal and explore the paths they took to get there.*
- **BEHIND THE SCENES:** *You'll need a Bible and a new shoelace for each person. Set up a challenge course with chairs and tables or boxes between starting and finish lines. Create the course so there's more than one path from the starting line to the finish. Place a Bible on a chair at the finish line.*

 **ACTION!** Form teams of up to five. Say: **Connect the feet of everyone on your team by tying them together with their shoelaces. You can attach shoelaces from shoe to shoe, gently wrap laces around team members' ankles, or whatever. When you're done, your entire team should be connected at the feet—no loose feet allowed!**

If some kids aren't wearing shoes with laces, provide laces for them to use. Next, explain to teams that their goal is to race through the challenge course to reach the finish. The first team to do that will win the race. If the race course is narrow, have teams go one at a time and time each team to see which was the fastest.

When teams are ready, start the race. After the

race, ask: **How did you like racing this way? How did you feel as you encountered the obstacles? How did you know which way to go? Were you trusting the person in front of you to lead you or did you keep your eye on the Bible at the finish line? Explain.**

CLOSE UP!

Assign one of these Scripture passages to each team: Matthew 2:1-12; Luke 2:1-7; and Luke 2:8-21. Have each team discuss the following questions: **Who was going to the manger? How did they know to go there? How did they get there? What did they do when they got there?** Have each team report to the large group. Then ask: **How have you come to Christ in your own life? How did you know to come to him? What happened when you came to him? Did you follow someone else or did you find your own path to Christ? Explain.**

It's a Wrap!

Distribute new shoelaces to the group. If kids are wearing shoes with laces, have them take out one lace and replace it with the new one. If kids aren't wearing shoes with laces, have them tie the laces around their ankles. Say: **However they got there, those who went to the manger were never the same again. They became new people. We, too, become new as we come to Christ. Let's be thankful this Christmas that Jesus came to us,**

so we could be changed by him.

Have the groups come together in a circle and hold hands. Go around the circle and have each person offer either a spoken or silent prayer, thanking God for the new life Christ has brought.

EASTER LIGHTS

- **TOPIC:** *Easter*
- **SCRIPTURE:** *John 16:16-22*
- **SYNOPSIS:** *Group members will go through a maze in the dark to experience what the disciples might have felt like when Christ was crucified.*
- **BEHIND THE SCENES:** *In a large room, set up a maze with chairs and tables covered with sheets. Make sure your maze has different paths to follow. Turn off the lights, then set a flashlight on its end so it shines on the ceiling.*

  In addition to the maze, you'll also need a Bible and an apple for each person.

 **ACTION!** Gather everyone at the start of the maze. Then say: **On "go," I want each of you to crawl through this maze. There will be a reward for those who reach the end.**

Turn off the lights, then say: Go!

 **CLOSE UP!** Reward everyone who finishes the maze by giving them each an apple. Turn on the lights, then ask: **How did it feel to be in the maze? How would you have felt if there had been no light at all to follow? Did you depend on someone else to guide you or did you try to find your own way?**

Read John 16:16-22 aloud. Ask: **How do you think the disciples felt when Jesus died? Why did they have trouble understanding what God's "big-picture plan" was for Jesus? How was the disciples' experience like going through this maze? What was the "light" they had to guide them through those dark days?**

Form groups of three. Ask group members to share a time they couldn't find any "light" to follow in life or a time when they had a hard time believing God could be in charge of the "big picture."

 **It's a Wrap!** Have the whole group form a circle. Set the flashlight in the center and turn out the rest of the lights. Say: **Even as the disciples struggled with the "why" of Jesus' death, God had planned a resurrection. Even in our darkest struggles, God is there holding an "Easter light" and saying, "I am with you. Follow me."**

Close with a prayer thanking God for always being the light in our darkness.

BEST DAD

- **TOPIC:** *Father's Day*
- **SCRIPTURE:** *Luke 15:11-32*
- **SYNOPSIS:** *Group members will write contemporary versions of the story of the prodigal son and discover that God is the perfect Father who can meet all their needs.*
- **BEHIND THE SCENES:** *You'll need Bibles, paper, and pencils.*

 **ACTION!** Form groups of no more than four and give each person a Bible, paper, and a pencil. Say: **Imagine that the Fox Network has decided to broadcast some of the dramatic stories Jesus told. But they want the stories put into contemporary settings for today's audiences. Your job is to write a screenplay for the story found in Luke 15:11-32. Be creative and work as a team but be sure each of you makes a copy. You'll have five minutes. Go.**

After five minutes, call everyone back together. If you have five or fewer groups, have each group act out its screenplay.

If you have more than five groups, have kids number off within their groups from one to four. Form four new groups by sending all "ones," "twos," "three," and "fours" to different areas of the room. Have kids take turns reading aloud their previous groups' screenplays.

CLOSE UP! After the screenplays have been shared, gather everyone together and have kids stand as you ask the following questions. Tell kids you'd like to hear lots of interesting responses. When one person shares an answer, kids who thought of the same answer and have nothing more to add can sit down. When everyone is seated, ask the next question and repeat the process.

Ask: **What went through your mind when you were putting this story into a contemporary setting? What words would you use to describe the character of the father? How would you feel about having a father like that? How does it feel to know that God wants to be that kind of father to you? How can having God as your father help you when you have problems with your own father or you don't have a father around? What encouraging things could you do this week to bring out the best in your parent?**

It's a Wrap! Ask each person to share one meaningful memory of his or her father (or a person who was like a father to them). As kids share, write down their responses on a sheet of paper.

When everyone has shared, say: **It's wonderful when we can have good times with our fathers. Those good qualities in our dads come from God. But even if we have bad fathers or are having rough times with our dads, we have a Father in God who can meet our needs. I'm**

going to lead us in a prayer thanking God for the way he fathers us.

Start the prayer by saying: "Thank you, God our Father, for..." Then read the memories kids shared, adjusting them as necessary so they'll apply to God. For example, "My dad helps me with my schoolwork" could become "Thank you, God, for helping me with my schoolwork."

HOW FAR WOULD YOU GO?

- **TOPIC:** *Good Friday*
- **SCRIPTURE:** *John 15:12-14*
- **SYNOPSIS:** *Group members will drive toy cars to explore their commitment to friends.*
- **BEHIND THE SCENES:** *You'll need a permanent marker and newsprint. Use masking tape to mark off 10 equal distances on a smooth floor. You'll also need a toy car, a Bible, paper, and a pencil for each person.*

**ACTION!** Give kids cars and have them put their cars behind the first line on the floor. Have kids move their cars to the next line for each of the following acts of friendship they would normally do.

Say: **Move your car forward one line if you**

would typically...

- greet your friends in the hall at school.
- share your lunch with a friend who forgot his or her lunch.
- give a friend money when asked.
- let a friend stay at your house when he or she is in trouble.
- stick up for a friend in front of other friends.
- confront a friend when he or she is doing something harmful.
- confront a friend when he or she is doing something illegal.
- give a friend your most prized possession to pay their debt.
- take the blame for a friend in trouble with the law.
- die for your friend.

After the kids have moved their toy cars, ask: **How far do you think friendship should go? What does a person gain by showing strong commitment to another? How do you feel when a friend asks you to do something that goes beyond your present level of friendship?**

 **CLOSE UP!** Have kids form teams of three or four to read John 15:13. Provide paper and pencils and have each team create their own "10 Levels of Friendship" based on the activity they just experienced. For example, a group might say, "Level 1 is the Acquaintance Level, because there's no commitment beyond just being friendly to one another." Make sure groups create headings and descriptions for all 10 friendship levels.

When the groups have finished, have them share their lists with the class, then have all the kids work together to make one list.

Copy the final list onto newsprint. Then ask: **How many friendships do you have on Level 10? Why do you think you have so few friendships on that level? What level of friendship do you think Jesus had for his disciples before his crucifixion? What level of friendship do you think Jesus has for you now? Explain.**

It's a Wrap! Pass around a permanent marker and have kids write the name of a friend and the number that corresponds to that person's present level of friendship on their cars. Form a circle and have each person say a one-sentence prayer for his or her friend.

Close by reading aloud John 15:12-14.

TARGETED IMPACT

- **TOPIC:** *Graduation*
- **SCRIPTURE:** *Matthew 28:19-20*
- **SYNOPSIS:** *Group members will receive a piece of a cross as a symbol of going out from the youth group to impact their world.*
- **BEHIND THE SCENES:** *Use a jigsaw to cut a*

large oak cross out of a 4-foot piece of a 1×12. Cut a small section for each kid out of the cross and drill a small hole into each section. Insert a key ring chain through the hole. Place the key rings in a paper sack. You'll also need a Bible. (You can use this devotion for graduations every year until the wooden cross is gone.)

**ACTION!** Place the wooden cross in the center of your room and have the kids gather around it. Read Matthew 28:19-20 aloud. Say: **You've each been a special part of our youth group and our church. You've made a difference in my life, in each other's lives, and in the life of our community. Now it's time for you to go out into the world to make an impact for Christ. This cross represents the impact our group will make on the world. You are part of that impact and, therefore, part of this cross.**

Give each graduate a key ring section that you've cut from the cross. As you hand each graduate a key ring, say: (Name), **you are part of our impact on the world. Use this key ring as a remembrance that you're a part of us, and we're a part of you.**

**CLOSE UP!** After all the graduates have received their key rings, gather the whole group together and ask: **How does it feel to be stepping away from the youth**

group? What words of advice would you offer to kids just now entering the youth group? How has God been a significant part of your life in the past few years? If you could change anything about your high school experience, what would it be? What's your greatest hope for the future?

It's a Wrap! Have the undergraduates gather around the graduates and volunteer to tell the graduates one positive way they've impacted the youth group. Make sure each graduate is affirmed before you close.

FREE INDEED

- **TOPIC:** *Independence Day*
- **SCRIPTURE:** *Galatians 5:1, 13*
- **SYNOPSIS:** *Group members will use sparklers to spell out what freedom means to them.*
- **BEHIND THE SCENES:** *You'll need a sparkler for each person. You'll also need a Bible and a lighter. Plan to do this devotion outside. Have a fire extinguisher close by in case of fire.*

 **Give each young person a sparkler.** As you light each sparkler, have each kid choose one word that describes what freedom means to him or her. Then have kids use their sparklers to spell out their words in the air—one letter at a time. Have the rest of the group try to guess every letter and word kids create. Continue until all kids' "freedom" words have been guessed.

 Afterward, read Galatians 5:1, 13 aloud. Ask: **Why did you choose the word you did? What does freedom mean to you? What does our freedom in Christ mean to God? What do you think God wants us to do with the freedom he's given us in Christ? How can you carry out God's wishes this week by serving others?**

It's a Wrap! Have kids form pairs and tell their partners how they could serve each other this week. For example, partners may decide to clean each other's rooms, bake cookies for each other, or pray for each other. Encourage kids to make commitments they'll carry out this week. Then have partners close in prayer together, thanking God for the freedom he gives.

MOM

- **TOPIC:** *Mother's Day*
- **SCRIPTURE:** *Proverbs 23:25*
- **SYNOPSIS:** *Group members will learn how they've made their mothers rejoice.*
- **BEHIND THE SCENES:** *You'll need paper, pencils, and Bibles. Contact group members' mothers and ask them to attend this devotion. If kids' mothers aren't available (or kids don't have a mother at home), have fathers or other significant adults attend. Ask the adults to think of three reasons they rejoice about their teenagers. For example, someone might say, "I rejoice that my son is so kind to others" or "I rejoice that my daughter's faith has grown so strong." Remind adults to choose only positive, joyful things to say.*

    ***Note:** It's possible that not all teenagers will be able to have a mother or other adult present. Be prepared to be a "stand-in mom" for these teenagers. You might also want to recruit other youth workers to be "stand-in moms" for kids.*

 **ACTION!** When kids arrive, have them prepare to write a letter of thanks to their moms. Encourage kids to remember the good things their moms have done for them during the past year.

While kids are working on their letters, invite the moms into the room. Have kids stop what they're doing. Then have the moms go to their teenagers and share the three joyful things they thought of.

Form groups of four or five consisting of moms and kids together, then ask the teenagers: **What was it like to have your mom say good things about you on Mother's Day? How does that feeling exemplify the way we should respond to our mothers? What surprised you most about what your mother said?**

 **CLOSE UP!** Have a volunteer read aloud Proverbs 23:25. Then ask the teenagers: **What kinds of things can our mothers rejoice about that we're already doing? What things can we do differently so our mothers will rejoice about our actions?** Let groups share their insights with the rest of the class.

Then ask the mothers: **What are reasons your children can rejoice about you? What things might you change so your teenagers will rejoice even more?**

It's a Wrap! Have each kid take a turn completing the following sentence in private for his or her mom (replace "mom" with "dad" or another word for those whose moms couldn't attend): "I'm grateful you're my mom because . . . " Have teenagers close the devotion by praying for moms everywhere.

BACK TO CLASS

- **TOPIC:** *New school year*
- **SCRIPTURE:** *Proverbs 13:4*
- **SYNOPSIS:** *Group members will learn that it pays to be diligent in schoolwork.*
- **BEHIND THE SCENES:** *You'll need supplies for making cookies (the more complicated the recipe, the better). Make sure you have enough supplies for two separate groups to work independently on making the same cookies. You'll also need Bibles.*

 **ACTION!** Form two groups. Say: **The object of this activity is to make delicious cookies. But both groups will go about the cookie making in different ways.**

Have one group be the Sluggard Souls and the other be the Diligent Drones. Tell the Sluggard Souls to goof off as much as possible while making the cookies. Tell them to ignore the recipe and make up their own. Encourage this group to have fun at the expense of making great cookies.

Tell the Diligent Drones to follow the instructions exactly and to not waste any time goofing off while making the cookies.

After the cookies are mixed, have kids taste both groups' cookie dough. Then ask: **What was it like to be in the Sluggard Souls? the Diligent Drones? Which group did a better job of meeting the goal of creating delicious cookies? Explain.**

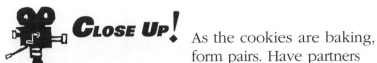

CLOSE UP! As the cookies are baking, form pairs. Have partners share one thing they're looking forward to and one thing they're dreading about the coming school year. Then have partners read Proverbs 13:4. Read aloud the dictionary definitions of "sluggard" and "diligent," then have pairs discuss the following questions: **What kinds of things would a sluggard do to prepare for and participate in school? What kinds of things would a diligent person do? Why is it important to be diligent in our work? What are the benefits of diligence at school? Can people be too diligent? Explain. How can you balance having fun at school with being diligent about the work?**

Say: **Approaching a new school year with an attitude of diligence can help you succeed. But diligence without an element of fun can ruin a year. It's important to find a proper balance of diligence and fun to succeed in school.**

It's a Wrap! As you enjoy the cookies, have kids tell each other one way they'll be diligent in the coming school year. This could be anything from "studying daily" to "paying more attention in class." Then have kids tell each other one way they'll have fun. Close by having partners pray for each other and the coming school year.

A NEW DAY

- **TOPIC:** *New Year's Day*
- **SCRIPTURE:** *Psalm 51:7-12*
- **SYNOPSIS:** *Group members will explore what it's like to make a new start in life.*
- **BEHIND THE SCENES:** *You'll need washable face paints, paintbrushes, mirrors, Bibles, washcloths, soap, and water.*

 **ACTION!** Form pairs. Have kids brainstorm ways they've disobeyed God or failed in other ways during the past year. These can be significant events, such as failing in school, or smaller events, such as yelling at a friend. Then have kids use the washable face paints to paint words or symbols onto their partners' faces symbolizing each of the events they've shared. For example, a poor school year might be represented by a big "F," or a bad attitude might be represented by drawing a face with a sneer.

Encourage kids to be honest about their sins and failures in the past year. When kids have covered their partners' faces, have volunteers stand before the whole group and answer questions about the symbols and words on their faces. Have mirrors available for kids to use during this time.

Then ask: **What does it feel like to have a face full of sin and failures? Why do we often dwell on our mistakes? What would you give to be able to start over and erase these failures?**

CLOSE UP! Form groups of no more than four and have kids look up Psalm 51:7-12 then discuss the following questions: **What feelings might the psalmist have been experiencing while writing this passage? How are those like the feelings you experience after looking back at mistakes or failures? What is it like to dwell on the things of the past? How did the psalmist expect to move beyond past sins and failures?**

Have kids take turns washing each others' faces using the washcloths and mild soap. Then have kids look at their clean faces in the mirrors. Ask: **How is the way you were cleansed of these symbols and words like the way God cleanses us of past sins? What does it take to make a new start in life?**

It's a Wrap! Form a circle. Have kids take turns holding a washcloth and praying for God to cleanse their sins and renew them for the coming new year. Then go around the circle and have kids say one positive thing they hope to do in the coming year that won't end up on a list of sins or failures.

TAKING CONTROL OF TEMPTATION

- **TOPIC:** *St. Patrick's Day*
- **SCRIPTURE:** *Psalm 119:105-111*
- **SYNOPSIS:** *Group members will discover that focusing on God makes it easier to control their actions in life.*
- **BEHIND THE SCENES:** *Using rope or heavy string, make one 36-inch "snake" for each person. You'll need two three- or four-foot sticks. You'll also need a Bible for each person.*

ACTION! Say: **Legend says that St. Patrick drove out all the snakes from Ireland many centuries ago. So for St. Patrick's Day, we're going to play a "snake" game.**

Form two teams and gather both teams at one end of the room. Set up a finish line at the opposite end of the room. Give each person a rope "snake." Hold up the sticks and say: **When it's your turn, use a stick to try to push your snake across the finish line, then run back to your team. Your next team member will do the same until your team has driven all your snakes to the other end of the room.**

There are two requirements in this race: 1) You must push only the snake's head or tail with the stick, you cannot push it from the

middle, and 2) if any part of the snake touch-
es you, you have to start over.

After teams have lined up, start the race. When
everyone is finished, congratulate kids on their
efforts. Then ask: **What went through your
mind as you tried to keep from touching the
snake while moving it away from your team?
How could you compare this experience to
avoiding sin when temptation strikes?**

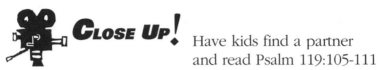 Have kids find a partner
and read Psalm 119:105-111
together. Have kids answer each of the following
questions with three or less words in their pairs:
**What can we do to find a way out of a tempting
situation? What help does God promise when
we find ourselves in danger? What can we
expect if we follow God's rules?**

 Have kids form a circle.
Take one of the sticks the
kids used for the race and say: **When we are
tempted, we can find help by looking to God.
As we pass this stick around our circle, pray a
one-sentence prayer for the person on your
right. You might pray that that person will
embrace God's strength, wisdom, and encouragement when facing temptation.**

SON SCREEN

- **TOPIC:** *Summer vacation*
- **SCRIPTURE:** *Ecclesiastes 11:7-10 and Colossians 3:17*
- **SYNOPSIS:** *Group members will simulate being protected by sunscreen then discuss how "screening" their activities through God's Son protects them.*
- **BEHIND THE SCENES:** *Blow up four yellow balloons. Place a strip of masking tape across the center of the floor. You'll need two bottles of sunscreen (preferably colored zinc oxide that shows easily on skin), Bibles, pencils, slips of paper, and one yellow balloon for each person.*

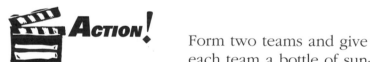 **ACTION!** Form two teams and give each team a bottle of sunscreen. Say: **Put sunscreen on a small area of your body—like an elbow, wrist, or your nose.**

Have the teams stand on opposite sides of the dividing line. Give each team two yellow balloons. Say: **These are "suns." You may touch the suns only with the part of your body that has sunscreen on it—otherwise you'll be incinerated. On "go," toss the suns in the air. Your goal is to get the suns to land on the other team's side. Your team may hit the suns as many times as needed, but no one person may hit a sun twice in a row. Go!**

Let teams play for three minutes, recording how many times the balloons hit the floor on each side.

CLOSE UP!◆ After the game, have the two teams move to the center of the room and face each other in two lines. Say: **The person facing you in the other line is now your partner. Discuss my first question with him or her. Then move one position to the left for a new partner and answer my next question. If you're at the left end of the line when it's time to move, go around to the other end.**

Ask: **How did you feel during this game? How did the dangers from the "suns" affect you? What are some real-life dangers you encounter when you're having summer fun?**

Have all the kids in one line read Ecclesiastes 11:7-9 aloud. Ask: **How does this Scripture relate to summer fun? What temptations seem especially strong during the summer? What are some of the dangers of giving in to those temptations?**

Have all the kids in the other line read Colossians 3:17 aloud. Ask: **How can Jesus be like sunscreen, helping you to enjoy your summer without getting burned?**

It's a Wrap!◆ Give everyone a yellow balloon, a pencil, and slips of paper. Say: **On your slips of paper, write an idea for a fun, God-pleasing summer activity**

and put the slip in your balloon.

When everyone has finished, have kids blow up their balloons. Say: **Take your balloon home. When you're looking for something fun to do this summer, pop the balloon and read the idea inside. And remember, God is in favor of fun, but he doesn't want us to get "burned."**

BUNCHES OF MEMORIES

- **TOPIC:** *Thanksgiving*
- **SCRIPTURE:** *Psalm 78:1-7*
- **SYNOPSIS:** *Group members will explore the value of common memories and give thanks for the group's experiences during the last year.*
- **BEHIND THE SCENES:** *You'll need several bunches of grapes. You'll also need a Bible for each person.*

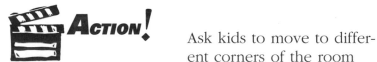 **ACTION!** Ask kids to move to different corners of the room depending on how they answer each of the following questions.

Ask: **Would you rather remember...**
- **a big family reunion, a quiet meal with close relatives, or a special time with two or three friends?**

● **a meal with lots of great food, a meal with fun company, or a meal with entertainment?**

● **a long trip to see family, a short trip to be with friends and family, or preparing for guests?**

After the questions, ask: **Which of these experiences we've described would make you feel the most thankful? Explain.**

 **CLOSE UP!** Have kids form clusters based on their responses to the last question. (If your group is small form one cluster.) Ask a volunteer in each cluster to read Psalm 78:1-7. Pass around the grapes and tell everyone to take some but not to eat them yet. After everyone has a handful of grapes, go around the cluster and have each kid share a positive memory of Thanksgiving as he or she eats a grape. Have kids do this for each grape they've taken. For example, kids might say, "We always have sweet potatoes" or "My Aunt Gertrude always makes gooseberry pie." When kids each get to their last grape, ask them to share a memory of something special that's happened in the youth group.

It's a Wrap! Form new clusters by having kids move to different corners according to how they answer this question: **In the youth group, do you prefer fun events, service events, or worship events?** Have each cluster pray together giving thanks for the special memories the youth group shares. If a cluster is small, encourage kids to share other youth group memories while waiting for the larger clusters to finish.

FILTERING OUT LOVE

- **TOPIC:** *Valentine's Day*
- **SCRIPTURE:** *1 Corinthians 13*
- **SYNOPSIS:** *Group members will compare the world's perspective on love with the love described in 1 Corinthians 13.*
- **BEHIND THE SCENES:** *You'll need newsprint, markers, and Bibles.*

 **ACTION!** Form groups of no more than four. Assign each group one of the following sentences: It took all of my savings, but I love my new car; Every time I'm around him/her I feel nervous—I think I'm in love; It's springtime and love is in the air; I love chocolate; What's so wrong about making love if you're in love with the person?

Say: **Spend the next five minutes thinking of a definition of love based solely on the usage of the word in your sentence. Begin your definition**

Looking at Our Special Days

with the phrase: "Love is something that . . . "

Allow five minutes for groups to explore their phrases, then have each group present their definition to the whole group. Ask: **Does any one definition adequately cover the concept of love? Why or why not? Why does the word love have so many meanings? What was it like to define love in such a narrow way? Based on these definitions, what is true love? How is the difficulty of defining the word "love" like the difficulty in understanding what real love is?**

 **C**LOSE **U**P**! ♦** Say: **To understand the true meaning of love, we have to go to the Bible and look at what Paul wrote in 1 Corinthians.**

Have volunteers take turns reading 1 Corinthians 13 aloud. Then have kids list on newsprint the elements that define love, such as love is patient, love is kind, and so on. Once the list is complete, have kids go back to their original assigned phrases and run them through the "filters" they just listed on the newsprint. Ask kids to see if these "usage" examples fit the definition of love from 1 Corinthians 13. Have volunteers share other ways people use the word "love." Run these through the filters, too.

Then ask: **Why is it so difficult to show true love to others? What are ways people show unselfish love? How have you been shown true love? How have you shown true love?**

It's a Wrap! Have kids each choose one filter from the newsprint that they need to develop most. Then have kids pray for each other to develop those filters in their lives.

Close by having kids thank each other for expressing specific filters of love within the group. For example, someone might say, "Tom, I've appreciated your patience with us in the group" or "Terri, you are the epitome of kindness in my life."

SCRIPTURES

Scripture Index